NEW JERSEY

A Photographic Celebration

Foreword

New Jersey is one family with many faces and a wonderful home. In photograph after stunning photograph, Walter Choroszewski truly celebrates the beauty of our people, the diversity of our communities, and the richness of our abundant natural resources. And what he articulates in images, the remarkable historian, John T. Cunningham, depicts in words. Their work continues to fill New Jerseyans with a tremendous pride of place and gives us ample reason to redouble our efforts to preserve our open spaces, our traditions, and our heritage for the generations to come.

— Governor Christine Todd Whitman

Any collection of photographs that truly celebrates the New Jersey we love must go beyond the picturesque shots of the Shore and the Pine Barrens, beautiful as they are. The essence of our New Jersey can only be captured by paying visual tribute to aspects of the state that we often take for granted but, which nevertheless, are woven into the fabric of our lives: Jersey Fresh tomatoes, Lucy the Elephant, and, yes, even toll booths! These pages evoke pleasant memories and beckon us to explore every corner of the Garden State.

—Governor Jim Florio

When I look at Walter Choroszewski's photographs, I am reminded of how easy it is to celebrate New Jersey. I have had the good fortune to experience the beauty, history, and personality of New Jersey. Every picture, whether it be a sunrise on the beach at Sandy Hook, a race at the Meadowlands, or a cranberry harvest in the Pinelands, recalls fond memories. One cannot look at these pictures and not marvel at our complexity. There is so much to celebrate and this book invites us to celebrate it—New Jersey's glorious past, present and future.

—Governor Tom Kean

Flying north from Washington in a small plane while the sun is setting, as I've so often had the occasion to do, you reach a point where the sunlight on the Delaware river turns it into a metallic-looking band extending all the way from Trenton to the Water Gap. There lying before you is the New Jersey Peninsula in all its magnificence. From the mountains of the northwest to the flat farmland of the south, New Jersey has so much to offer. With this diverse collection of beautiful photographs, Mr. Choroszewski truly captures the essence of the Garden State.

—Senator Bill Bradley

I will never forget one glorious day when I was boating down the Great Egg Harbor River. Although the surrounding forest is thin, there is a stark beauty in this place where woods and river and sky blend together like the colors on an artist's palette. During the trip, I witnessed a truly magnificent sight. An eagle flew overhead— its power and grace evidenced by its impressive wing span and its seemingly effortless movement. The bird reminded me of the abundance and beauty that New Jersey has to offer. This book invites everyone to come and discover its richness for themselves.

—Senator Frank R. Lautenberg

Half Title. *Springtime view from Sunrise Mountain in Stokes Forest, Sussex County.*

4-5. *Flag Plaza at Liberty State Park, Jersey City.*

NEW JERSEY
A Photographic Celebration

WALTER CHOROSZEWSKI

Introduction By

JOHN T. CUNNINGHAM

Foreword By

GOVERNOR CHRISTINE TODD WHITMAN - GOVERNOR JIM FLORIO - GOVERNOR TOM KEAN

SENATOR BILL BRADLEY - SENATOR FRANK R. LAUTENBERG

Published By

AESTHETIC PRESS, INC.

SOMERVILLE, NEW JERSEY

With love, for Susan and Joe

NEW JERSEY, *A Photographic Celebration*

ISBN   0-933605-06-4
Library of Congress Catalog Card Number: 96-86342

AESTHETIC PRESS, INC.
P.O. Box 5306, North Branch Station
Somerville, NJ 08876-1303
Tel: 908 369-3777

In Celebration of New Jersey

An Introduction by

John T. Cunningham

Let the flags flutter boldly in the winds that sweep across Liberty State Park; let the trumpets blare, the bass drums boom, the cymbals clang. There is no better place to begin celebrating that place called New Jersey than within the very shadow of the Statue of Liberty; this world-renowned statue, although claimed by our neighbor, is in New Jersey, more than a half mile west of the New York border.

It is neither provincial nor chauvinistic for New Jerseyans to celebrate their state in all its varied moods, fascinating geographic diversity, distinctive changing of seasons and its many national groups that now call New Jersey home.

Everyone who leaves the dull, if bustling, New Jersey Turnpike knows of New Jersey's natural beauty—the parks that brighten urban Essex County, the broad hardwood forests that spread across northern New Jersey, the dense Pine Barren of southern New Jersey and the mile after mile (127 miles, indeed!) of the sun-touched white sand called the Jersey Shore.

New Jersey offers so much to celebrate. The state's motto, Liberty and Prosperity, tells of a state that is proud of its freedom and riches—a state rich in history, blessed with natural resources, and a diverse population that has found prosperity in many places and ways. From harvesting the fertile farmland to fishing the bountiful sea. All along New Jersey's rivers, canals and spillways sprang up countless mills—Walnford Mill, Prallsville Mills and Cooper Mill, to name a few— all generating commerce and prosperity.

Beaches, mountains, lakes, and swamps; cities, suburbia, villages and farms— New Jersey is a visual cornucopia. Fortunately, we have Walter Choroszewski as our "designated photographer" to capture on film our state's delights. While Choroszewski has all the technically sound cameras, lenses, and equipment necessary, he, more importantly, has the "eye"—that innate ability to look at a scene and find "art." He also knows just the right moment to "push the button," capturing the image forever.

Choroszewski has the patience to wait, hours if need be, until the sun sifts through the fog lifting over the Delaware River at Milford. He tarries until the billowing flags at Liberty State Park open fully with the sun's clear light illuminating our nation's colors. He lingers with the gulls until the setting sun reaches exactly the right warm glow over Barnegat Bay.

In this, his fifth book showcasing the beauty of New Jersey, Walter Choroszewski shows that nothing—not snow, not rain, nor heavy fog thwarts him. He makes weather his ally, his conveyor of moods. But he also has the uncanny luck of finding crystal blue skies, rainbows and warm sunrises to light his way across New Jersey. Walter

6. Prallsville Mills,
along the Delaware & Raritan
Canal towpath, Stockton.

Choroszewski travels far beyond the pathways of most New Jerseyans. He knows where the cranberries cover the waters like a red carpet, where spring-fed streams gush down steep green hillsides, and where brilliant yellow goldfinches sing in the meadows. His love of nature is well-evidenced within this book.

As we turn the pages of this colorful and exciting portrayal of our state we encounter the people of New Jersey celebrating "life" at the state's many festivals and events. We see the skies filled with balloons soaring over Hunterdon County. We hear the drummers beating African rhythms at a Garden State Arts Center Heritage Festival. And we thrill at the graceful dancers performing "The Nutcracker."

New Jersey's place in history is woven throughout this volume. We are taken from the shores of the Delaware River where General George Washington made his historic Christmas crossing, to Washington Park in Newark where a statue of the General stands in silhouette against the urban skyline. Images of the Holocaust Memorial in Liberty State Park and the New Jersey Vietnam Veterans' Memorial in Holmdel, remind us of recent history as well.

Jersey tomatoes, horse shows, and boardwalk amusements—these are some of the most familiar symbols of our state. But New Jersey aficionados also know the landmarks that are vintage New Jersey—Ford Mansion, Barnegat Lighthouse, Waterloo Village, the Old Red Mill, and the thundering Great Falls.

For the past four decades I also have seen the classic images and have trod the same New Jersey off-the-beaten paths that Walter Choroszewski has taken. I have brought back innumerable impressions etched on my brain or written in scores of note pads; however, Choroszewski's advantage lies in "film"—images that are immediate and enduring. Share in Walter's personal "Celebration" of New Jersey through this special collection of photographs.

—John T. Cunningham

7. *Towpath Tavern along the old Morris Canal at Waterloo Village.*

John T. Cunningham, as a journalist, author and historian, is one of New Jersey's leading ambassadors of state pride. An alumnus of Drew University, Cunningham's career in journalism dates from notable years with the *Morristown Record* and the *Newark News*, to publishing over twenty-five books on the state, including high school and elementary texts. John has been a long-time resident of Florham Park in Morris County.

New Jersey, *A Photographic Celebration*

*F*or my first book on New Jersey, which I photographed in 1980, I was told to make the state "look like New England," and I was told that it would likely be a daunting task. As I crossed the George Washington Bridge into New Jersey and traveled down Route 95 to the entrance of the New Jersey Turnpike, I stopped to take my first photos for this assignment—the swaying grasses that filled the ancient lake bed of glacial Lake Hackensack, today's Meadowlands.

That first assignment never ended, as today I continue to drive the highways and byways (not necessarily the New Jersey Turnpike), traveling almost a half million miles throughout New Jersey, in search of images that celebrate my adopted home state.

The images in this collection were photographed mostly through the mid-1990s, with some personal favorites from my early years also included. The photos were taken on a variety of camera formats ranging from 35mm to 4x5, in natural light with slow-speed color reversal films including Kodachrome, Ektachrome, Fujichrome and Fuji Velvia, and many photos required the use of a sturdy tripod.

In the years I have been photographing this state, I have discovered that it is certainly <u>not</u> New England. It is New Jersey—an entity with a beauty and charm that is uniquely its own: a peninsula between two great rivers containing mountains, rolling hills, pine barrens, a fertile coastal plain and miles of shoreline along the mighty Atlantic. It is also the many interesting people I have befriended along the way: the fishermen, the dancers, the cowboys and the artists. People of different ethnic backgrounds and traditions, families, seniors and especially the children—who will always remain "forever young" in these photographs.

—Walter Choroszewski

As a photographer, author and lecturer, Walter Choroszewski has been enhancing New Jersey's positive image through his numerous photographic books and calendars since 1980. His photography is widely published in editorial, corporate, and advertising publications, and his fine art prints appear in many corporate collections. A graduate of Penn State University and a native of Pennsylvania, Choroszewski moved to New York City where he began his career in photography, and later settled in New Jersey in 1985. The Choroszewski family—Walter, Susan, Joe and "Beans", their English Springer Spaniel—lives in rural Somerset County.

9. *Lily pads decorate a Pine Barrens waterway in Wharton State Forest.*

10. *Autumn reflections in Speedwell Lake, Morristown.*

11. *Remnants of historic Weymouth Iron Furnace, Atlantic County.*

12-13. *Evening lift-off at the New Jersey Festival of Ballooning, Solberg Airport, Readington.*

14. *Jersey City's modern skyline, opposite the World Trade Center on the Hudson River.*

15. *Sunset glow behind the Liberty Science Center, Liberty State Park.*

16. *Dawn's glow over the Lido Diner on Route 22 in Springfield, Union County.*

17. *A New Jersey Transit train on the Bergen Line leaves the station at Ridgewood.*

18. *Early morning
walk along the beach
at North Wildwood.*

19. *"Show us your shoes!"
Atlantic City's annual
Miss America Parade.*

20. *Springtime aerial of Broad Street and the village of Hopewell.*

21. *Spring greens surround the Delaware & Raritan Canal at Griggstown.*

22. *Rolling waves on the beach at Sandy Hook.*

23. *Ballet dancers perform "The Nutcracker" at the State Theater in New Brunswick.*

24. *Colonial highway marker found at the Demarest House in historic River Edge.*

25. *Early morning sunlight illuminates a flag in front of brownstones in Hoboken.*

26. *The Holocaust Memorial at Liberty State Park in Jersey City.*

27. *Veterans pause to remember, at the New Jersey Vietnam Veterans' Memorial in Holmdel.*

28. *The Old Cotton
Mill bell on display at
Wheaton Village in Millville.*

29. *Autumn's golden
color borders the Rahway
River through Cranford.*

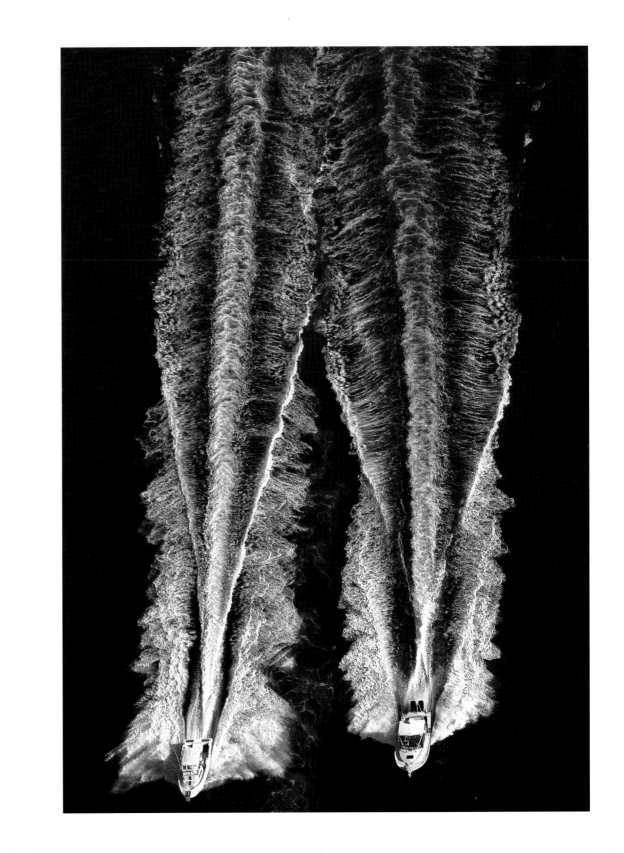

30. *"Surfs up"*
along the Jersey Shore
at Manasquan.

31. *Power boats ply*
the Intracoastal Waterway
near Manahawkin.

32. *Cherry trees border the stream in Branch Brook Park, Belleville.*

33. *The Moon Gate within the Chinese Garden at Duke Gardens, Somerville.*

34. *Fly fishing at the Ken Lockwood Gorge on the South Branch of the Raritan.*

35. *A blanket of leaves covers the General Store at Ralston, Chester Township.*

36. *Buttermilk Falls*
tumble down the steep slope
of the Kittatinny Mountain.

37. *September goldenrod*
adds color to the dunes at
Cape May Point State Park.

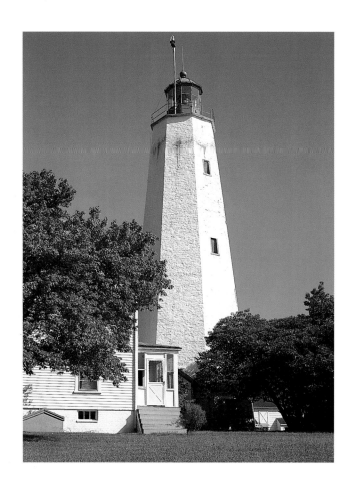

38. *Some of New Jersey's magnificent lighthouses. Left to right: Sandy Hook Lighthouse, Absecon Lighthouse, Cape May Lighthouse.*

39. *The century-old Victorian-style Sea Girt Lighthouse.*

40. *A family of drummers at the Black Heritage Festival, The Garden State Arts Center.*

41. *"The South Jersey Promenaders" perform at a wine harvest festival.*

42. *A stream of lights traverses the Delaware Memorial Bridge in Salem County.*

43. *A Roebling-built pedestrian bridge spans the Delaware River at Bull's Island D&R Canal Park.*

44. *Ripe Norton grapes on the vine at Renault Winery in Atlantic County.*

45. *An inviting mural welcomes all to Amalthea Winery in Camden County.*

46. *Footprints lead to the ocean at Cape May Point.*

47. *Making summer memories at the beach in Bay Head.*

48. *Cowboys watch the action at Cowtown Rodeo in Salem County.*

49. *Country music fills the air during "Millbrook Days".*

50. *Student transportation parked under the arches at Princeton University.*

51. *A blur of bicycles race at the annual, "Tour of Somerville".*

52. *Beach grass sways in the breeze on the dunes of Island Beach State Park.*

53. *Traditional Indian dancing at a festival in Essex County.*

54. *Warm afternoon light on the War Memorial near City Hall in Jersey City.*

55. *Morning fog rises from the Delaware River at the bridge in Milford.*

56. *Late November reflections*
in the Wanaque River,
Ringwood State Park.

57. *A Jacquard Loom*
at the Paterson Museum
in "The Silk City".

58. *Gulls rest on the pier over the bay at Mantoloking.*

59. *Seniors enjoy the day at Sunset Beach in Cape May Point.*

60-61. *Split rail fencing and autumn foliage near the Tempe Wick House in Jockey Hollow.*

62. *The gilded dome of America's second oldest State House, Trenton.*

63. *The State Seal in the*
General Assembly Chamber of
the State House, Trenton.

64. *6 AM at a Washington Township farm, Morris County.*

65. *A misty farm sunrise near Neshanic, Somerset County.*

66. *Inquisitive looks over a fence in Cokesbury.*

67. *An October Sunday morning in Grandin, Hunterdon County.*

C.A. ROTHENGLE LOG HOUSE
THIS PROPERTY IS REGISTERED ON THE
NATIONAL LIST OF HISTORIC SITES BY
THE U.S. DEPT. OF THE INTERIOR
BUILT 1638–1643

68. *New Jersey's oldest log home in Gibbstown, Gloucester County.*

69. *Clapboard patterns on the wall of the sawmill at Batsto Village.*

70. *The Henry Rutgers Baldwin Gate at Rutgers University in New Brunswick.*

71. *Morning light bathes the cliffs of the Palisades, Bergen County.*

72. The Captain shows us a prize "New Jersey" lobster caught in the cold Atlantic.

73. A successful catch in the surf at Point Pleasant Beach.

74. *Dawn's light on the Hackensack River at New Bridge Landing.*

75. *Porch columns of the Steuben House in River Edge, Bergen County.*

76. *Racing fans*
fill the stands at the
Meadowlands Racetrack.

77. *"And they're off!"*
Harness Racing at
the Meadowlands .

78. *A wind surfer at Spruce Run Reservoir, Hunterdon County.*

79. *Workers pass crates of produce at the Vineland Farm Auction.*

80. *Running down the stretch
at the annual Monmouth County
Hunt Race Meeting.*

81. *Awaiting their turn
at the Gladstone Driving Event
in Somerset County.*

82. *Home lights shine on Schooley's Mountain near Hackettstown.*

*83. Stained glass colors
dance on the walls of the
University Chapel, Princeton.*

84. *Casino lights glow at
Park Place in Atlantic City.*

85. *The Wallace House–
Washington's headquarters
in Somerville.*

86. *James Fitzgerald's*
"Fountain of Freedom"
near Woodrow Wilson Hall,
Princeton University.

87. *The boys of Bayonne*
cool off in the fountain
at Dennis Collins Park.

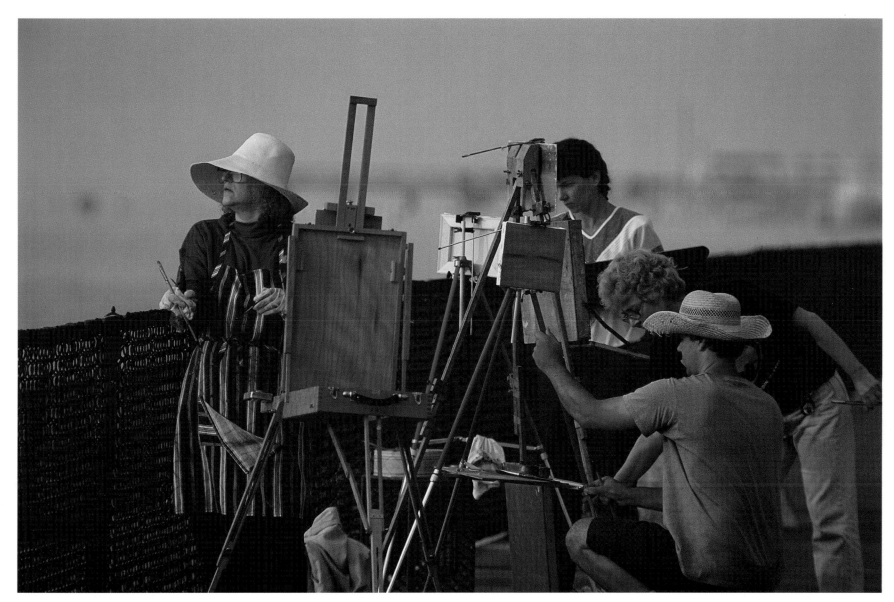

88. *The pink light of dawn on the dunes of Barnegat Light.*

89. *Morning art class on the boardwalk at Point Pleasant Beach.*

90. *Historic Cooper Mill,
on the Black River in Chester
Township, Morris County.*

91. *A mill chase
runs through Little York,
Hunterdon County.*

92. *Rolled hay in the*
fields of an Amwell Valley
farm, Somerset County.

93. *An Earth Day*
clean-up crew in the
Ironbound section of Newark.

94. *Tending to the nets at Point Pleasant.*

95. *Sunset over the Maurice River in Cumberland County.*

96. *A fresh snowfall caps the*
Green Sergeant's Covered Bridge
on the Wickecheoke Creek.

97. *The Hunterdon*
Historical Museum, featuring
the "Old Red Mill", Clinton.

98. *Bed & Breakfast Inns along Gurney Street in Victorian Cape May.*

99. *Spring tulips bloom near the Emlen Physick Estate in Cape May.*

100-101. *View of Highlands, Sandy Hook, and beyond, from the Twin Lights of Navesink.*

102. *Morning sun breaks over Mt. Tammany in the Delaware Water Gap.*

103. *Delaware Indian "Lone Bear" visits Indian Island at Waterloo Village.*

104. *Fresh peaches at
a farmstand in Tabernacle,
Burlington County.*

105. *Fruit preserves
at the Hermitage in
Ho-Ho-Kus, Bergen County.*

106. *Awaiting the judge's decision at the Gloucester County 4-H Fair.*

107. *"Lucy"—still on patrol at the beach in Margate, Atlantic County.*

108. *Hobie cat races
in the sea off Wildwood.*

109. *Sailboats race with
the wind on Lake Hopatcong.*

110. *Homegrown "Jersey tomatoes"*
and basil, South Branch.

111. *Local competition is intense*
for the New Jersey Championship
Tomato contest, at a Somerville
weigh-in station.

112. *The Friends
Meeting House in the
town square of Crosswicks.*

113. *Church steeples
rise above the quaint river
village of Lambertville.*

114. *The Walnford Mill along Crosswicks Creek in Monmouth County.*

115. *Brookdale Farm in Port Murray, Warren County.*

by Land, Sea and Ai...

116. *An annual tradition:
The 4th of July Parade in
Lebanon, Hunterdon County.*

117. *Watching the Independence
Day fireworks display over
Hillsborough High School.*

118. *A brick pathway leads to Ford Mansion, Washington's Headquarters at Morristown.*

119. *Water tumbles over moss-covered rocks in Worthington State Forest.*

120. *Silhouette of the General at Washington Park in Newark.*

121. *High Point Monument pierces the sky atop Kittatinny Mountain.*

122. *Nassau Hall,*
Princeton University.

123. *Old Queens,*
Rutgers University.

124. *The Great Swamp National Wildlife Refuge in Morris County.*

125. *A Pine Barrens bog near Chatsworth, Burlington County.*

126. *Tubing down the Delaware River at Kingwood, Hunterdon County.*

127. *Canada geese versus the Princeton Women's Crew on Carnegie Lake.*

128. *Aerial view
of Brielle and the
Manasquan River Inlet.*

129. *Waiting for the
charter fishing boats to
pass at Avon-By-The-Sea.*

130. *Toll booths at Exit 14 of the New Jersey Turnpike.*

131. *View from the ferris wheel at Mariner's Landing in Wildwood.*

132. *Harvesting the*
cranberries begins at
dawn in the Pine Barrens.

133. *Cranberries*
float on the surface at
Double Trouble State Park.

134. *New Jersey's symbols.*
Left to right:
Eastern Goldfinch,
State Seal on the flag,
Violet.

135. *Students from a*
Bridgewater-Raritan school
compete at the State House with
their entry for the State Song.

136. *The Federal-style mansion at Barclay Farmstead in Cherry Hill, Camden County.*

137. *The Annual Garden at the New Jersey State Botanical Gardens at Skylands.*

138. *The Pine Creek Railroad steam train at Allaire State Park.*

139. *Monorail service between the terminals at Newark International Airport.*

140. *The Christmas Day reenactment of Washington crossing the Delaware.*

141. *The Battle of Monmouth reenactment at Monmouth Battlefield State Park.*

142. *An autumn ride along Surprise Lake, Watchung Reservation.*

143. *Horse show and competition at the Flemington Fair.*

144. *River-Lea Farm, Branchburg, Somerset County.*

145. *Still Meadow Farm, Branchburg, Somerset County.*

146. *The East Point Lighthouse in Heislerville is a beacon on the Delaware Bay.*

147. *Nautical flags welcome all seafarers to Perth Amboy, Middlesex County.*

148-149. *The glittery casino skyline of Atlantic City reflects in Forsythe National Wildlife Refuge.*

150. *Oyster shells at Bivalve, Cumberland County.*

151. *Standing at the top of Great Falls, Paterson.*

152. *Fallen leaves along Old Mine Road, Sussex County.*